Dubai

The 30 Best Tips For Your Trip To Dubai – The Places You Have To See

Traveling The World

brands within this book are for clarifying purposes only and are the owned by the owners themselves, not affiliated with this document.

Contents

Introduction

Welcome!

First, I want to thank you and congratulate you for downloading 'Dubai Travel Guide: The Ultimate Dubai Travel Guide for Tourists and Travelers – The Top 30 Amazing Places to See and Things to Do in Dubai'.

The content within this travel guide has plenty of information on how you can get the ultimate experience when you go about travelling to the beautiful city of Dubai. In this guide, you will learn almost everything you need to know about the wonderful city of Dubai.

This travel guide will serve as your bible when you go to prepare your tour around the whole of Dubai. Before we go any further, I want you to accept that Dubai is considered one of the most amazing cities on Planet Earth and you'll surely understand why once you are there. This guide is written for anyone who wishes to travel to Dubai and who is seeking the full Dubai experience.

It's stressful for some people travelling to another region and equally stressful in the planning. With this travel guide, you'll find yourself well prepared than otherwise to go to Dubai and you'll find it easy to enjoy yourself as well.

What I am hopefully trying to achieve in this travel guide is to provide you with a very dependable travel guide on exactly what you should see and do when you are in Dubai.

Thanks again for downloading this ebook, I really hope that you will enjoy it and that it'll help you along your journey. With all that being said, let's get started!

The Timeline of Dubai

First of all, I think it'll be a good idea for you to know the wonderful timeline of this great city. The following are major events that have occurred in Dubai and amongst its people.

Origins

Even after finding various artifacts during excavations, it's hard to determine the earliest periods of Dubai with certainty. The city is located along the coast which was very influential on the city. Fishing became a major part of the economy. It also served as a major port city for the Middle East where trade began to develop here.

Before Oil Discovery

Along with Dubai's fishing industry, it also became known for its pearl trade industry. These two industries were the main drivers of the Dubai economy. The Great Depression had a big effect on the economy and the crash cause hardship on the city.

Oil Boom

Oil was discovered in Dubai after it's neighbor Abu Dhabi became a popular place for finding oil. After the first oil field was uncovered, a large boom in the oil industry occurred in Dubai. This drove a lot of foreign workers to the city to begin developing this lucrative industry. This was around the same time of the city developing its infrastructure to support a growth in population such as an airport and bridges.

Modern Dubai

Dubai has grown rapidly after the oil discovery. The entire city rose up from the ground with skyscrapers, apartments, office buildings, and more. The wealth that Dubai has attracted has transformed it into a dream vacation destination for people all around the world. The current city that you see has been developed since the late 1900s.

Geography and Climate

Geography

Dubai is located on the Persian Gulf coast. Its elevation is right at sea level. Over the course of history, sand has receded, resulting in the current coastline and land area of the city. It's also in the Arabian desert. Much of Dubai's original landscape was sand which has since been developed on.

Climate

Dubai shares its climate with the rest of the Arabian Desert. All year round it has very hot and dry temperatures. During the summer months, daily highs can easily be over 40 °C (or about 100 °F). Even in the winter months, Dubai still experiences hot days full of sunshine. There is very little precipitation with high humidity.

Dubai Culture

Dubai is a very beautiful city. Over the years, it has grown rapidly attracting foreigners for work and vacation. The Dubai culture is developed from the overall culture in the United Arab Emirates which can be seen in their sports, music, architecture, arts, food and music.

Population of Dubai
There are approximately 3 million people that live in Dubai. This number consists of so many expats that only less than 20% of the population accounts for national Emirati people. Many of these expats come from Asia, with India having the highest number of people living in Dubai.

Languages of Dubai
The official language in Dubai is Arabic, which is the national language of the United Arab Emirates. English is the second official language and is widely spoken. Dubai has a major tourism industry which utilizes predominantly English. Various Asian languages are used in various communities based on where they originated.

Religion in Dubai
Islam is the official religion in Dubai. The Islamic religious practices have shaped much of the cultural heritage of the United Arab Emirates. Dubai has many large mosques which are managed by the government. With Dubai's diversity, you'll also find almost every other religion around the world. Christianity is another common religion. People are allowed to practice other religions as well as have religious buildings built in Dubai.

Art in Dubai
Much of the art in Dubai has been influenced by Islam as well. Islamic art is very common around Dubai. This style

of art is characterized by repeating patterns and geometric shapes. It extends across various art methods including painting, embroidery, glass, and even calligraphy.

Sports in Dubai

Dubai is a very popular place for great sports teams. Football is the most popular sport in Dubai. Dubai has several different football clubs and is known as a city with the best teams in the world. They have often competed for the FIFA World Cup trophy. Cricket is also a very popular sport in Dubai with several large stadiums around the city. Other more regional sports include falconry and camel racing.

Architecture in Dubai

Dubai has a mix of architecture styles. On one side, you'll see a lot of older, traditional buildings from Dubai's early days. On the other side of the Dubai Creek, you'll see some of the most modern buildings in the world. Many of the style choices of the buildings on either side can be traced back to Islamic influences of the architecture.

Music in Dubai

The traditional music in Dubai stems from Arabic music. This is the staple music of the entire Middle East region. Dancing often accompanies many of the popular traditional songs. Dubai has now become a very popular place for modern day musicians to perform. Many high level performers have performed in Dubai in almost every genre. Dubai also hosts different music festivals.

Food in Dubai

Dubai is one of the best places to enjoy food from all around the world. Arabic cuisine is the traditional dish of Dubai. Arabic food is typically served with a wide variety of dishes with rice, frequently incorporating chicken, lamb, and other meats. Since Dubai has such a diverse population, you can find food from lots of different cultures including Indian, Chinese, Malaysian, and much more.

Holidays in Dubai

Dubai officially recognizes all of the holidays following the Islamic religion. Two of the major holidays include National Day, on December 2nd, which marks the formation of the UAE. Also the holiday of Eid ul-Fitr, which is the end of Ramadan.

Things to See and Do in Dubai

Dubai is filled with numerous of fascinating attractions and offers a deeply diversified culture. As Dubai is one of the most exciting cities in the world, I want to suggest to you a list of things you should see and do during your time in Dubai. You may want to research further into them as you prepare for your trip.

See the Top of the World at the Burj Khalifa

What is the Burj Khalifa?
The Burj Khalifa is currently ranked as the tallest building in the world. It towers over 800 meters high above the city of Dubai. It was completed in late 2009 and is one of the most iconic buildings in the world. This skyscraper is part of a largest development called Downtown Dubai. It consists of projects including the largest landmarks in Dubai.

The Burj Khalifa was designed by the firm SOM, who is also credited with designing the One World Trade Center in New York City and the Willis Tower in Chicago. The design is influenced by Islamic architecture practices and pulls design elements from mosques and other Islamic towers around the world. The Burj Khalifa includes a hotel, suites, residential apartments, a restaurant, and office space.

Visiting the Burj Khalifa
No matter where you are in Dubai, you'll be able to see the Burj Khalifa. It's one of the most recognized buildings in

the world and a staple of the Dubai skyline. It's the most famous attraction in the city.

The biggest reason that people visit the Burj Khalifa is for its observation deck. The entire building has 163 floors with the observation deck being on the 148th floor. From this high above the ground, the experience appropriately is named "At the Top". The observation deck gives amazing views over all of Dubai. With high visibility, you'll even be able to see Iran in the distance. The deck has a unique viewing telescope with AR technology. You'll be able to see the real-time view of Dubai as well as special views of the city in different scenarios such as weather conditions and time of the day.

Experience the Luxury of the Burj Al Arab

What is the Burj Al Arab?

The Burj Al Arab is a five-star hotel in Dubai. Its name translates into 'Tower of the Arabs'. Many people even call it the world's first seven-star hotel because of the level of luxury incorporated into the hotel, from it's architecture to the hospitality service or even just the small details that they attended. This is the third tallest hotel in the world and one of the most luxurious. Ever since it was opened at the end of 1999, it has become one of the most recognized symbols of Dubai.

Visiting the Burj Al Arab

The Burj Al Arab is an exclusive hotel to stay in while visiting Dubai. It was built on an artificial island in the Persian Gulf which is accessed by a single road. It even has a helipad on the roof to transporting wealthy individuals to and from the hotel. There are a couple restaurants located within the hotel. Since it's located off of the city's shores, you'll be able to dine with amazing views of the Dubai skyline. Although it's one of the tallest hotels in the world, there are only a couple hundred rooms and suites. The most expensive room has a rate of over $20,000 per night.

Shop, Play, and Entertainment in the Dubai Mall

What is the Dubai Mall?

The Dubai Mall is another complex incorporated in the Downtown Dubai development project. It was built adjacent to the Burj Khalifa. Just as the Burj Khalifa is the tallest building in the world, the Dubai Mall is the largest mall in the world. It's currently at a size of over 13 million square feet and is currently being expanded.

The Dubai Mall is a one stop shop for almost anything you can image. The mall holds more than 1,200 shops. In addition to the shops, there are other attractions in the mall including: hotel, cinema, the Dubai Aquarium, an indoor theme park, a kids' park, an ice skating rink, and over 100 restaurants and cafes.

Visiting the Dubai Mall

The Dubai Mall is one of the must-see attractions when you visit Dubai. This mall is much more than a shopping center and can provide a lot of added entertainment to you trip to the city. The mall is located in the same downtown complex with the Burj Khalifa and the Dubai Fountain, amongst other landmarks. They are actually connected via the metro link so it's easy to go between two of these popular Dubai destinations.

You'll need plenty of time to browse the amount of shops located in the mall. Since tourism is such a major part of the Dubai economy, you'll see many western world brands ranging from high end fashion brands to smaller boutique shops. The Dubai mall is also the home of the Dubai Shopping Festival.

Go Skating at the Dubai Ice Rink

What is the Dubai Ice Rink?

The Dubai Ice Rink is an Olympic-sized ice rink found on the ground floor of the Dubai Mall. This is one of the more popular activities and entertainment found here. It's a destination for all ages. Both locals and tourists frequent think skating rink. The skating rink is large enough to accommodate large parties so there is plenty of room to maneuver around the rink. Whether you're an experienced skater or a first-timer, you can find a way to have fun here.

Visiting the Dubai Ice Rink

No need to worry about bringing equipment. Skates and other equipment is provided for you at the Dubai Ice Rink. There is staff and coaches available to assist with skating if needed. In case you don't want to skate and just watch, there is seating room around the skating rink. Not only is it a destination for the leisure activity, but you can also catch a variety of events here. There are ice shows, competitions, and ice hockey games that take place here. There are also special family events with music to create a fun skating atmosphere. On days with events, access to the ice rink may be limited.

Walk the Boardwalk of the Dubai Marina

What is the Dubai Marina?

The Dubai Marina is a man-made canal that runs through Dubai. It's a district that stretches more than 2-miles. On either side of the canal you'll see towering skyscrapers. Many of the buildings currently present in the Dubai Marina district are residential buildings which create a waterfront community in the desert environment. There are plans to expand the marina to incorporate a variety of buildings. This will eventually be considered the "Tallest Block in the World". It will be numerous skyscrapers and towers ranging from residential to commercial space.

The Dubai Marina is known for its Dubai Marina Yacht Club. It's where you'll find the Marina Boardwalk as well as the Dubai Marina Mall.

Visiting the Dubai Marina

You can easily access the Dubai Marina via the metro link which has a station right in the center of the marina. The Dubai Marina is an impressive sight considering that the entire canal was artificially built. You may even occasionally see sharks or whales swimming through the marina because of the proximity to the Persian Gulf.

The Marina Boardwalk is a popular pastime for both tourists and locals. You'll have amazing views of the marina and the surround skyscrapers. You'll also be able to see the diverse mix of yachts that dock here. The Dubai Marina Mall is another large mall in Dubai, although not at the scale of the Dubai Mall. You'll still be able to browse between over 100 retail shops.

Watch the Dubai Fountain Water Show

What is the Dubai Fountain?

To accompany the rest of the world-record developments in the Downtown Dubai development, you'll come across the Dubai Fountain, the largest choreographed water show in the world. It's located in the Burj Khalifa Lake, a 30-acre artificial lake built at the foot of the Burj Khalifa. The Dubai Fountain stretches more than 75 meters long and has the capability to shoot water more than 150 meters high, or 50-stories. The fountain was designed by WET Design, who also designed the famous water fountain show t the Bellagio Hotel in Las Vegas.

The Dubai Fountain opened simultaneously with the Dubai Mall opening ceremony. Special technology is used in the fountain to animate the dancing water which is set to lights and music.

Visiting the Dubai Fountain

There is a lot to see and do in Downtown Dubai and the Dubai Fountain is always the top of visitors' bucket list to see. The show lasts just a few minutes and is set to a variety of music and light coordination. There is a long list of music and water choreographies so each time you see it could give you a different viewing experience. Also depending on where you stand when you view it. The Dubai Fountain show can be seen from anywhere around the Burj Khalifa Lake. For an even more unique viewing experience, you can visit any of the nearby restaurants with viewpoints or even from the observation deck of the Burj Khalifa.

Hit the Slopes at Ski Dubai

What is Ski Dubai?

Ski Dubai is one of Dubai's premier theme parks. It's an indoor ski resort located right in the Mall of the Emirates, another major shopping mall in Dubai. This ski resort is entirely made-made, creating a realistic but artificial environment to enjoy skiing right in the middle of the desert.

The centerpiece of Ski Dubai is the mountain reaching 85 meters high. There is a lift that takes visitors up the mountain. There are 5 different ski slopes that you can enjoy. Each slope has different characteristics such as height, difficulty, and more. There are also rails, kickers, and boxes on each slope that get rearranged daily so you have a different riding experience each time you come.

Visiting Ski Dubai

Ski Dubai is an attraction that you wouldn't expect to find in a place like Dubai but they literally thought of everything when developing this great city. The entire park includes of 20,000 square meters of ski area as well as a Snow Park. The Snow Park is located next to the ski mountain and is a area to enjoy other wintertime activities such as giant snowballs, icy body slides, and even an ice cave to explore. At different times throughout the day, real life penguins get released into the park where you have opportunities to interact with them.

Ski Dubai is a destination for skiing and snowboarding. The park provides any equipment you may need for the slopes or you can but your own at the ski shop.

Cool Off at the Aquaventure Waterpark

What is the Aquaventure Waterpark?

Aquaventure Waterpark is considered the best waterpark is the Middle East. It's an outdoor waterpark located in the famous Atlantis hotel. It's claim to fame is the Aquaconda, the world's largest waterslide.

Aquaventure Waterpark is a park to enjoy for all ages and is very family friendly. The park consists of many different features. You can see everything from waterfalls to enjoying a private beach that extends into the sea.

Visiting the Aquaventure Waterpark

There are a variety of experiences that you can have at the Aquaventure Waterpark. You can spend your time lounging on the sunbeds that line the beach. Or you can take part in the water fun of the park. The Tower of Neptune is a notable area of the waterpark. Here, you'll find water rides and rollercoasters. This park also includes a special shark safari. This safari gives you the rare opportunity to actually swim with sharks and sting rays. In case you need a break from the water, there is a restaurant located in the park that services international food and drink options.

The Aquaventure Waterpark creates the perfect tropical atmosphere from the weather to the design of the park's décor. Since Dubai is in the middle of the desert, this will be the perfect way to cool off from the heat. To accompany the refreshing experience of the waterpark, you'll also have a great view of the Dubai skyline.

Spend a Day at Jumeirah Beach

What is Jumeirah Beach?

With Dubai located along the coast, Jumeirah Beach is the perfect place to visit, lining the Persian Gulf sea. This beach is located within the Jumeirah District of Dubai, where its name was derived from. The beach is characterized with white sand and clear blue waters. It's maintained well and a very clean beach. It's a place for lounging in the sun or cooling off in the hot, desert heat.

Jumeirah Beach is lined with commercial and residential establishments. There are numerous hotels, resorts, and other residential accommodations with great views overlooking the beach. There is also a shopping complex here or you can stop by some of the other individual shops, restaurants, or cafes located here.

Visiting Jumeirah Beach

Jumeirah Beach is where a lot of visitors go to escape the desert environment of Dubai. It's a beach where all ages can find enjoyment. There is even a bouncy castle in the water for kids to enjoy. The newest addition of Jumeriah Beach is the Ferris wheel, although the entire area is still being developed.

The beach is fairly large with plenty of space to stretch out. There isn't much natural shade that you can find along the beach but you can rent sunbeds and umbrellas in case you plan to be there for a while.

You'll find all the typical beach activities here to enjoy in or out of the water. It's also an ideal spot to view the beautiful Dubai sunset.

Discover History in the Dubai Museum

What is the Dubai Museum?

The Dubai Museum is the official museum of Dubai. It's located in Old Dubai, in the Al Fahidi Fort, the oldest building in Dubai. It was originally built in 1787 but converted into a museum in 1971. The Al Fahidi Fort was established to help protect the city from land advances from enemies and also serve as a prison. Even though it's a museum now, it still maintains its original aesthetic.

The Dubai Museum was set up to showcase Dubai's history, culture, archaeology, and information about the fort. It's a historical site in itself with plenty to learn. The entire fort surrounds an outdoor courtyard. The fort halls have been converted into various galleries. These galleries include renditions of various traditional Dubai scenes: The Creek, mosques, farms, and houses.

Visiting the Dubai Museum

The Dubai Museum will provide a major contrast of the city. From the location to the different exhibits, you'll be able to learn the timeline of Dubai, from the early years of the fort, to the modern metropolis that you see today. There are tours or your can walk through the exhibits self-guided. The tours last between 30 minutes to one hour so it's a fairly small museum with lots of information.

You'll be able to see life-sized replicas and representations of traditional life in Dubai. From replica food stalls, to different instruments that were played. There are even original objects from the fort such as the cannons located in the courtyard. After browsing through the museum, your can buy souvenirs at the gift shop.

Experience the Religious Significance of the Grand Mosque

What is the Grand Mosque?

The Grand Mosque is an iconic building located in the Old City of Dubai. This landmark is located next to the Dubai Museum. It was originally built in 1900 as a school to teach the Quran. It was demolished then rebuilt, then further renovated over several years and completed in 1998 to the current building you see today.

The Grand Mosque is a symbol of Dubai's religious and cultural heritage. It's one of the largest mosques in Dubai and the Middle East overall. The mosque consists of two parts. The main mosque and the minaret. The Minaret is the tallest minaret in Dubai, towering 70 meters above the ground. The mosque holds a capacity of 1,200 people.

Visiting the Grand Mosque

A very important thing to keep in mind before visiting the Grand Mosque is that it is a religious building so different rules apply to it as compared to some of the other major tourist attractions in Dubai. The main rule is that only Muslims are allowed into the main mosque. This is done to preserve the religious context of the mosque and allow space for prayer. Visitors are more than welcome to enter the minaret or walk the grounds of the mosque. Photography is even allowed.

Another big rule for visiting the Grand Mosque is the dress code. No shoes are allowed and specific clothing must be worn, especially for women. In case you forget to dress appropriately, you can buy appropriate clothes nearby.

Witness Traditional Life in Heritage Shindagha Village

What is Heritage Shindagha Village?

Heritage Shindagha Village, or just simply Heritage Village, provides a glimpse into the historic Dubai. It is located in the historic Al Shindagha neighborhood which is the perfect setting for such an attraction.

Heritage Village was created in 1997 with a purpose of preserving the traditional life in the UAE. It provides visitors an immersive experience into what life was like before modern skyscrapers lined the Dubai skyline. There are tours available that take you throughout the village to see up close the traditional lifestyles that were found in Dubai.

The Emirates maritime history is one of the prominent lifestyles on showcase in Heritage Village. Also the traditions of Pearl Diving and the lifestyle surrounding these type of workers.

Visiting Heritage Shindagha Village

When you arrive at Heritage Village, it will be as if you are teleported into the historic Dubai. This is an actual village that has been preserved and renovated to maintain the true atmosphere of the Old City. The village is currently inhabited by residents so you'll mainly be looking at the architecture and set up of the village to get an idea of how Dubai used to be.

There are a variety of things to see in Heritage Village. There is an example of a Bedoin village, an armory with old weapons, and other traditional artifacts and tools that were used in the past. There is an on-site restaurant where you can even find traditional Dubai food.

Visit the Record-Breaking Dubai Aquarium

What is the Dubai Aquarium?

The Dubai Aquarium and Underwater Zoo are a duo attraction located in the Dubai Mall. It's classified as the largest suspended aquarium in the world. The attraction includes three main sections, the aquarium tank, aquarium tunnel, and the underwater zoo. When you visit the Dubai Aquarium, you'll get to see all three together as you make your way through the attraction.

There are more than 140 different species that can be found in the aquarium and numerous of each. These marine creatures swim throughout the 10-million liters that fill up the aquarium tanks. There are common and rare water creatures that are seen here. There's a variety of fish, amphibians, and reptiles. The Dubai Aquarium provides a great viewing experience as well as an educational experience to learn more about the animals here.

Visiting the Dubai Aquarium

Many people find themselves attracted to the Dubai Aquarium since it's visible from the outside in the mall. This only gives a view of the main large tank but to see the rest of the aquarium ad underwater zoo you have to enter. There are thousands of marine animals that are sectioned into their natural habitat environments. The underwater zoo is divided into different zones, the Living Ocean, Rocky Shore, and Rainforest. Some of the animals visible here include sharks, rays, penguins, seahorses, jellyfish, and much more. A recent addition to the aquarium is the King Croc, an animal more than 200 years old and the largest of its kind in the world.

Enjoy the Thrill of IMG Worlds of Adventure

What is IMG Worlds of Adventure?

IMG Worlds of Adventure is the world's largest indoor amusement park. It's also Dubai's first themed indoor amusement park which opened in the Summer of 2016. The entire park covers an area of 1.5 million square feet. It consists of four special themes: Marvel and Cartoon Network for the international brands as well as Lost Valley – Dinosaur Adventure and IMG Boulevard. Each of the themed sections of the park provide their own unique attractions and shops.

IMG World's of Adventure welcomes more than 10,000 visitors every day and is continuously growing. There are a total of 17 rides across the entire park which includes roller coasters, thrill rides, and other attractions based on popular attractions. Some of the most notable features of the park are the animatronic dinosaurs and the world's largest Ben 10 store, a themed character store in the Cartoon Network section of the park.

Visiting IMG Worlds of Adventure

You'll have a lot of ground to cover when you visit IMG Worlds of Adventure. Not only can you enjoy the various rides here, but also different themed retail stores, dining restaurants, and even a cinema. Each of these are tailored to the section that they are found. Each has its own special offerings including some live themed shows, 3-D, and even 5-D experiences. This theme park can be fun for all ages. For kids too young or too small to ride the main rides, there is also a designated kids section for them to enjoy.

Take a Trip Along Sheikh Zayed Road

What is the Sheikh Zayed Road?

The Sheikh Zayed Road is the main highway in Dubai that actually connects all of the emirates in the UAE together. It's the longest road in the UAE with a length of over 500 kilometers. It was completed in 1980 but later extended to its current length. The official name when talking about the entire road is the E 11 Highway, but it is referred to as different names depending on the city. It stretches from Abu Dhabi to Ras al-Khaimah.

Visiting the Sheikh Zayed Road

Any time you are traveling around Dubai, either to different attractions or traveling to one of the other nearby emirates, chances are you will end up on this road at some point. This road is so common that many of the modern Dubai skyscrapers and luxury hotels have been built along this road. You'll pass by tall blocks of buildings as you ride this road through the city. One of the main metro lines runs parallel with this road as well. Even with its size of seven to eight lanes on either side, traffic actually flows smoothly. It's a fast and easy way to get around Dubai.

Have a Family Outing at Mushrif Park

What is Mushrif Park?
Dubai has many public parks located around the city. Towards the east you will come across Mushrif Park, one of the largest public parks in Dubai. Mushrif Park is over 1,000 acres of green space, a big contrast to the surrounding desert landscape. It was built in the 1980s and refurbished throughout the years. There are always new additions to the park.

Mushrif Park has lots of amenities. There are areas for cooking out, swimming, shopping, or playing sports. There are also a variety of kids' playgrounds where they can have fun on rides, swings, and much more. It's a destination that families go to enjoy a day outside.

Visiting Mushrif Park
Mushrif Park is open daily for visitors to enjoy. There is a small entrance fee but you'll have access to the entire park. You'll also have to pay a fee if you plan on swimming in the pool.

Many people like visiting this park for a place of relaxation and spending time with your family. It's a popular place for picnics and other gatherings. There is plenty to do to keep you entertained for the entire day. Some of the common activities here include cycling, golfing, basketball, and football. There are also a variety of restaurants, shops, and cafes. You'll even find a mosque located within the park.

Island Hop Along the Dubai Waterfront

What is the Dubai Waterfront?

The Dubai Waterfront is a long term project to expand the city of Dubai into the Persian Gulf. While it is still a long way to go before being completed, parts of the waterfront are already in place to get an idea of where the project is going. When completed, it will be the holder of two world records: the largest waterfront in the world and the largest man-made development in the world.

The Dubai Waterfront is a collection of islands designed in the shape of an iconic Islamic symbol, the crescent and star. Each of these islands will be artificially made. It is planned to be over 130 million square meters into the sea. It will include commercial and residential properties as well as resorts.

Visiting the Dubai Waterfront

Although a majority of the Dubai Waterfront isn't completed, you can get a good idea of the development by visiting the Palm Islands. These are also artificial islands that are finished how the remaining waterfront will be. The waterfront will actually surround the largest of the Palm Islands, which is the largest man-made island in the world already.

The Dubai Waterfront will support 1.5 million people in its various venues. There are plans to develop an entirely new section of Dubai on this waterfront. It is a series of canals and islands that will be connected via various modes of transportation. This waterfront also gives easy access to he international airport.

Shop the Dubai Gold Souk

What is the Dubai Gold Souk?

The Dubai Gold Souk is a large gold marketplace found in the Old City of Dubai. A souk is a traditional market and this one specializes in Gold. It's found in the Deira district alongside a few other marketplaces. The Gold Souk is one of the largest and major attraction for tourists.

There are close to 400 retailers selling a variety of gold items. It's estimated to have over 10 tons of gold present in this marketplace at one time. There are both indoor and outdoor spaces for shopping. The entire marketplace consists of narrow aisles to walk between vendors and shops. There are goldsmiths, retailers, and much more. You can also find other items such as herbs, spices, and clothes.

Visiting the Dubai Gold Souk

Tourists are always impressed by the amount of gold found within the Dubai Gold Souk. Feel free to visit whether you have plans to buy gold or just simply walk through and see the sights. Everything is sold here, including gold bars, jewelry, figurines, and even more exotic gold items. You can choose a ready-made item or even inquire about getting something custom made. At all the retailers in this market, haggling on the price is expected. With so many options of shops, if you don't get a good price at one, chances are you can find a similar piece at another vendor.

Stimulate Your Senses at the Dubai Spice Souk

What is the Dubai Spice Souk?

The Dubai Spice Souk is another major souk, or traditional marketplace in Dubai. It's located in the Deira District directly next to the Gold Souk. This is a traditional Arab spice market where lots of shops and vendors sell a mix of spices and herbs from different regions in the Middle East and Asia.

The Dubai Spice Souk, or simple Old Souk, is characterized by narrow walkways with shops on either side. There are both indoor and outdoor sections of this marketplace. There are also many other items that you can find for same here including textiles, rugs, artifacts, household goods, perfumes, and teas. Although this is a well known place to visit for tourists, it's not as active as it used to be in the past due to more modern shopping options for similar items.

Visiting the Dubai Spice Souk

The Dubai Spice Souk is located in one of the older districts in Dubai. Walking through this souk is reminiscent of how Dubai used to be. At times, this can be a bustling marketplace with large crowds squeezing through the aisles to find the best deals. The price of everything for sale here is negotiable. It's mainly a destination for tourists so the initial prices can be much higher than what they will actually sell it for.

One of the best parts about visiting the Dubai Spice Souk is the experience for your senses. The entire souk is filled with exotic scents and a general colorful scenery.

Stroll Through the Historic Al Bastakiya

What is Al Bastakiya?

Al Bastakiya represents the historical district in Dubai. With Dubai's rapid development, much of the original appearance of Dubai has been converted into the modern metropolis but there are still places to get the original essence of the city such as this. Al Bastakiya is also referred to as the Al Fahidi Historical Neighborhood.

This district was first established in the late 1800s. In the late 1900s, a large portion of it was renovated for modern office buildings. Many of the houses were used for foreign workers who were working on the new projects. The rest of the district was actually ordered to be destroyed but a late decision was made to preserve it. It is now being renovated and restored to its original appearance.

Visiting Al Bastakiya

The Dubai Creek divides Dubai in the modern side and the old city. This Old City section of Dubai showcases the traditional way of life in the city. Visiting Al Bastakiya is like taking a walk through the past. The layout of this historical district consists of maze-like alleys that wind throughout the buildings. Even though it's historic, you'll still see a lot of activity going on here. There are a variety of shops, galleries, and even courtyards for lounging.

It's a popular tourist destination and you'll come across many other landmarks and places to visit while in the Al Bastakiya district. This includes Dubai's oldest building, the Dubai Museum, the Sheikh Mohammed Centre for Cultural Understanding, and the Al Fahidi Fort.

Swim with Dolphins in Dolphin Bay

What is Dolphin Bay?

Dolphin Bay gives you the opportunity to swim alongside dolphins. You'll find this attraction at the Atlantis Hotel. The Dolphin Bay is a dolphin habitat that is open to visitors to get up close and personal with the majestic creatures.

There are different experiences that you can have at Dolphin Bay, providing different levels of interaction with the dolphins. The Dolphin Encounter is the first level. It allowed you to play with the dolphins in shallow water. This includes touching, kissing, hugging, etc. The next level is the Dolphin Adventure. This is a more immersive experience with the dolphins where you'll be in deeper water to be able to actually swim with the dolphins. The next level is the Royal Swim. This gives you a full swimming experience with multiple dolphins. The most advanced level is scuba diving on an underwater adventure with the animals.

Visiting Dolphin Bay

Dolphin Bay is a tourist experience for all ages. Different levels of interaction with the dolphins is done to be able to accommodate young kids and even visitors with little or no swimming experience. The Dolphin Encounter is perfect for everyone while the scuba diving experience is only reserved for licensed scuba divers.

All equipment is provided such as the required wetsuits. There are plenty of opportunities for photos, either professionally with the Dolphin Bay experience or personally from a separate viewing platform. You will also get to learn more about the dolphins.

Visit the Floral Paradise of Dubai Miracle Garden

What is the Dubai Miracle Garden?

The Dubai Miracle Garden is a floral oasis in the middle of the desert. Ever since opening on Valentine's Day in 2013, the Dubai Miracle Garden has become a major attraction in Dubai. It is the largest natural flower garden in the world. The entire garden covers an area of more than 70,000 square meters, hosting over 100 million flowers. This garden has been awarded several awards.

The most impressive features about the Dubai Miracle Garden is the types of floral arrangements. The garden is filled with objects that are made from, or completely decorated with flowers. This includes trains, airplanes, birds, and even a giant functional floral clock. There are several other sights within the Dubai Miracle Garden such as the butterfly garden, an aromatic garden, retail stores, and mosques.

Visiting the Dubai Miracle Garden

The Dubai Miracle Garden is a destination for an outing with the family or a romantic destination for couples. The large garden has plenty of sites to see and walk around. This is an award winning garden for great reason.

Weather plays a major role in the Dubai Miracle Garden. It's impressive to have an attraction such as this in the desert which makes it even more exciting to visit. It's only open from October to April because of the weather. The entire garden is also maintained using filtered and recycled water for maintenance. Every year, the garden is redecorated with a new theme to give you a unique experience with each visit.

Enjoy the Wildlife in Dubai Safari World

What is Dubai Safari World?

Dubai Safari World blends a zoo experience with a theme park experience to create the current safari park attraction. This site replaced the former Dubai Zoo which closed in late 2017. There was always plans to renovate the old Dubai Zoo which was around for about 50 years before closing and reviving itself as the Dubai Safari World. While it is still in development to its ultimate goal, it is open for visitors to see the current progress.

Dubai Safari World covers an area of over 100 hectares of land. The park is divided into four main areas: Arabian village, African village, Asian village, and a open Safari village. The animals found in each respective village and overall environments are designed to mimic the real thing. There are approximately 2,500 animals of 250 species total. This number continues to increase with each stage of development.

Visiting Dubai Safari World

Although the Dubai Safari World is in its early stages of development, there is still plenty to see and do at this attraction. There are plans to make it one of the top five parks in the entire world and they are on track to do so.

This park is great to visit for all ages. It's an eco-friendly park for the benefit of the animals. Tours are arranged to take visitors throughout the park via buses. There is also an interactive program for kids for educational purposes about the safari.

Bird Watching at the Ras Al Khor Wildlife Sanctuary

What is the Ras Al Khor Wildlife Sancturary?

The Ras Al Khor Wildlife Sanctuary is a wetland reserve. Birds migrate here in large flocks throughout the year. It is one of the last few urban protected areas in the world. While modern Dubai and the Old City already have a large contrast, this wildlife sanctuary adds a bit more to the mix of sceneries in Dubai. With the rapid development of the city, the Dubai Municipality designated this region as off limits and sectioned it off from the public to help preserve it.

Visiting the Ras Al Khor Wildlife Sanctuary

The Ras Al Khor Wildlife Sanctuary is currently being developed to support more visitors. It's tricky to preserve the natural essence of the ecosystem while still inviting tourist to come for viewing, bird photography, educational purposes, and more. The most iconic bird of the sanctuary is the flamingo. There are several other species of birds, small mammals, and fish that you can discover here. It currently has bird viewing platforms where you can see the animals in the natural habitat undisturbed. The entire protected area is over 1,000 hectares and one of the few experiences to see pure nature in Dubai.

Explore the Dubai Motor City

What is Dubai Motor City?

If you're a motorsports enthusiast, then you'll enjoy the Dubai Motor City development. This neighborhood covers an area of 3 square kilometers. It was established in 2004 as a center for motorsports. The entire neighborhood is based on this theme. Included within this neighborhood are commercial properties, residential units, sports facilities, retail shops, a theme park and more. Because of the scale of the project, it is still in development.

There are 5 main features that make up Dubai Motor City. The Dubai Autodrome is a certified 5 kilometer motorsports circuit that has already hosted several major races from around the world. Uptown MotorCity is a collection of residential apartments to form its own community. This community even includes schools, parks, and other recreational activities. The Green Community MotorCity is another residential community developed here. It's more exclusive and includes villas, townhouses, and luxury apartments. The Business Park MotorCity contains office and retail space. It also holds various car showrooms and shops. And finally, the F1-X Dubai Formula One theme park.

Visiting Dubai Motor City

Dubai Motor City is located on the outskirts of the main Dubai city center. Public transportation isn't easily accessible here but you can easily find a taxi to travel back and forth to the other tourist attractions in Dubai.

Although there are still lots of projects to be completed for Dubai Motor City, you can still find a big selection of retail outlets, supermarkets, and restaurants.

Play in the Dubai Desert Safari

What is the Dubai Desert Safari?

The Dubai Desert Safari is considered one of the top experiences in Dubai. Seeing as Dubai is in the middle of the desert, this is one of the most popular attractions for visitors. Desert Safaris are conducted by a variety of tour providers. This experience takes you deep into the desert where you can take part in a variety of activities depending on what you want to do.

There are various experiences that you can choose between. A morning desert safari will let you see the beautiful sunrise from the desert dunes. You'll then be able to ride along the dunes on quad bikes, dune buggies, go on a camel ride, sand ski, and more. This experience typically will last up until lunchtime. An evening desert safari is the exact opposite. You'll be taken into the desert just before the sunset. You can relax you'll be able to go on a camel ride, enjoy dinner at the campsite, and even be treated with a belly dance show. An overnight desert experience is an extension of the evening desert safari. You'll be left at the camp overnight to be able to witness the sunrise in the morning. In case you don't want to be active, you can just opt for having dinner in the desert.

Visiting the Dubai Desert Safari

Each tour provider has similar desert safari experiences. They ensure that you have fun by taking care of logistics such as transportation to and from your hotel, food, amenities, and much more.

Place Your Bets at the Meydan Racecourse

What is the Meydan Racecourse?
The Meydan Racecourse is a large racetrack for horses located in Meydan City, Dubai. This racecourse opened in early 2010, replacing an older racetrack that was also located here. It has been the site of many major horse races internationally. The Dubai World Cup, for example, is the premier event, and is the richest racing event in the world with tens of millions of dollars in prize money. There are also plenty of other racing events that occur here. The racing season lasts annually from November to March.

Outside of the normal racing season, the Meydan Racecourse is still an active site. There are several other venues located here. It includes the first five-star trackside hotel. There is also a horse racing museum, a golf course, and restaurants.

Visiting the Meydan Racecourse
Visitors come to the Meydan Racecourse for both business and pleasure. The actual horse races are a favorite pastime for locals and tourists in Dubai. There grandstand can hold more than 60,000 people. Outside of the races, the Meydan Racecourse continues to bring people here all year round for different business activities and conferences. It's located away from the Dubai city center so it provides a different type of luxury for its guests. Other forms of entertainment include music concerts from major touring artists. There are always activities going on here. This is a great place to visit with your family to attend an event or for business outings.

Take a Swing at the Dubai Creek Golf and Yacht Club

What is the Dubai Creek Golf and Yacht Club?

The Dubai Creek Golf and Yacht Club comprises of two venues. It is a championship golf course which features an 18-hole par 71 course. It is also features the Yacht Club which opens out into the Dubai Marina. It's located in the center of the city in the Deira district.

The Dubai Creek Golf Club has a very distinct clubhouse building which is shaped like sails to a boat. Since being established in 1993, it's the most popular golf course in Dubai. It held the first golf academy in the entire Middle East. It has also hosted various international golf tournaments. The Yacht Club is held in a separate building which features restaurants, event venues, and a boardwalk stretching out onto the Dubai Marina.

Visiting the Dubai Creek Golf and Yacht Club

Both of the venues of the Dubai Creek Golf and Yacht Club can be enjoyed even without actually being a member. Service is the exact same in how you're treated by the staff and different amenities that you'll find at each location. The golf clubhouse features several rooms for preparing for the course including locker facilities and even a practice course. Everything is provided for you such as golf clubs, buggy, and other amenities.

For those who are actually members of either club, the site includes close to 100 villas for residents and even a large hotel.

Catch a Show at the Dubai Opera

What is the Dubai Opera?
The Dubai Opera consists of two portions. The main Dubai Opera house which is a multimedia performance venue, as well as the overall Opera District. This section of the city is located in Downtown Dubai nearby to many other tourist attractions. It's a cultural hub because of the various activities that are found here.

The Dubai Opera opened in August 2016. It hosts a variety of shows including opera, theatre, ballet, concerts, exhibits, and conferences. The max capacity of the venue includes seating for 2,000 guests. The interior is rearranged depending on the type of show or event is taking place. Stepping outside the doors of the Dubai Opera will bring you to the Opera District. This district includes many other cultural venues including museums and art galleries. It also has hotels, residential accommodations, retail shops, and recreation sites.

Visiting the Dubai Opera
The Dubai Opera hosts shows all year long. Some of the shows are local productions while others may be internationally traveling shows. Tickets can be purchased before arriving or onsite. There is plenty of staff readily available to assist with selecting a show, finding seats, and more. There is an onsite restaurant that you can dine at before or after your show. This performance arts center has shows and events that range is required ages. The Opera District also features various events and festivals throughout the year.

See the Picture Perfect Scenery Through the Dubai Frame

What is the Dubai Frame?
The Dubai Frame is one of the newest landmarks in Dubai, which opened at the beginning of 2018. This unique attraction is literally a picture frame giving you a framed view of modern Dubai and the Old City. It is unofficially recognized as the biggest picture frame in the world. It's located in Zabeel Park, in the middle of either side of Dubai. Depending on which side you stand will give you the contrasting views of Dubai.

The Dubai Frame was conceived as a result of an international architecture design competition. Over 1,000 proposals were fielded from around the world to create a new landmark to represent Dubai. The ironic thing about this landmark is that it's symbolic. Instead of creating another landmark, it was build to highlight the current landmarks of the city.

Visiting the Dubai Frame
The Dubai Frame is a great opportunity for photos of Dubai, both new and old. It's a dynamic frame because as new developments continue in the city, the resulting picture will change as well. Not only can this attraction be enjoyed from the outside, there is also an interior portion of the frame.

On the ground floor is a museum highlighting the culture of the United Arab Emirates. There a displays of traditional life in the region's past. After learning a bit of the history, you can take an elevator up to the top of the structure. Its height of 150 meters gives great views of either side of the city in addition to the see-through glass floor.

Conclusion

To conclude this entire travel guide, I want you to know that it will be your ultimate and quite memorable experience in your life when you go visit and tour around this iconic city of Dubai. I want you to know that this city has much value in store for you and that the only thing you need to leave behind when you go about visiting this city is to leave all your stress and worries back at home! For you to do so, you must follow and take in everything that consists in this travel guide.

I also really do hope that this book has enlightened you in some way. This book was specially written to help you understand Italy and all its attractions and wonderful things to do there. It can also be taken with you for use on your journey.

Also, if you enjoyed reading this book or find that this book holds some sort of value, then it would be very much appreciated if you could leave a positive review on to this book. I wish to reach to as many tourists and travelers who are planning to visit this great city of Dubai for the best of memories and times, and by you leaving a positive review, it will surely help me accomplish that. You might even gain some massive good karma!
And once again, thank you very much and the best wishes to you and your journey! Cheers!